223
12/96

HOLIDAY ITEM

One week loan
Limited number per card

7 DAY BOOK	THIS BOOK MAY BE KEPT FOR 7 DAYS ONLY, IT CANNOT BE RENEWED.

CHRISTMAS

	DATE DUE	
DEC 27 1996		

The NUTCRACKER

RETOLD BY
DAVID FREEMAN
ILLUSTRATED BY
JOANNA ISLES

PAVILION

A BIG THANK YOU TO LISA FROM ROSEBUD
FOR ALL THOSE WONDERFUL LUNCHES

First published in Great Britain by
PAVILION BOOKS LIMITED
26 Upper Ground, London SE1 9PD

A CIP catalogue record for this book is available from the British Library.

ISBN 1 85793 545 4

Set in Bembo
Printed in Hong Kong by South China Printing Co.

2 4 6 8 10 9 7 5 3 1

This book can be ordered direct from the publisher. Please contact the Marketing
Department. But try your bookshop first.

TO
HATTIE
LOTTE ★

It was Christmas Eve.

Fluffy snowflakes had been falling all day, turning the grey streets into a white wonderland. As the sun went down, the snow reflected candlelight from every window in the town.

Through the window of Clara's house a sumptuous Christmas tree, decorated with hundreds of candles, sent shafts of light into the night air.

Clara and her brother Fritz were having a grand party. They watched in awe and amazement as the guests arrived.

Clara was looking for one very special guest, her much-loved godfather, Herr Drosselmeyer. She knew he would bring her a remarkable present, and he had promised to provide some intriguing entertainment for the party. He had already sent a golden

Christmas angel by messenger. The angel had pride of place on the very top of the Christmas tree.

More guests arrived, but still there was no sign of Herr Drosselmeyer. Where could he be? Why was he so late?

'He has to come,' thought Clara, trying to keep her eye on the door. 'He promised.' Then she saw him.

Herr Drosselmeyer was famous as a clock-maker and inventor of magical toys. There had been a plague of mice in the palace of a nearby kingdom and he had designed a trap which had removed most of the unwelcome visitors. This made the Queen of the Mice so angry she cast a spell on his young nephew. The handsome young man was turned into an ugly Nutcracker doll. To break the spell the Nutcracker had to fight the fearsome

Mouse King, and despite his ugliness, a beautiful girl had to fall in love with him.

When Clara caught sight of her godfather, his kindly smile reassured her that this was going to be a memorable party. His smile broadened when he saw his angel at the top of the tree, but nobody noticed the special glance he gave her. They were all too busy gazing at the puzzling packages he had brought with him.

Herr Drosselmeyer opened the boxes to reveal two dolls as big as real people. When he wound them up, they began to dance around the room. The guests were entranced by this astonishing sight.

When the music stopped it was time for Herr Drosselmeyer to distribute his presents.

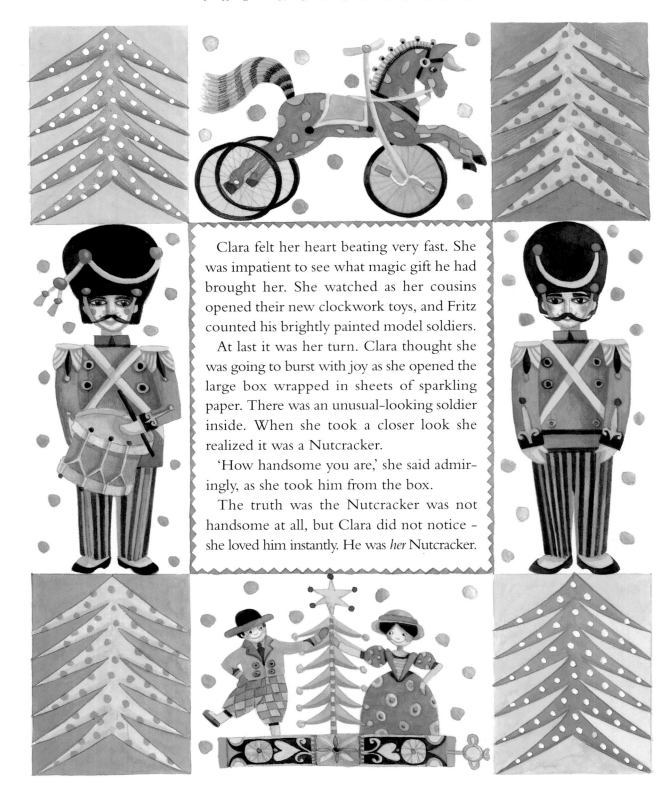

Clara felt her heart beating very fast. She was impatient to see what magic gift he had brought her. She watched as her cousins opened their new clockwork toys, and Fritz counted his brightly painted model soldiers.

At last it was her turn. Clara thought she was going to burst with joy as she opened the large box wrapped in sheets of sparkling paper. There was an unusual-looking soldier inside. When she took a closer look she realized it was a Nutcracker.

'How handsome you are,' she said admiringly, as she took him from the box.

The truth was the Nutcracker was not handsome at all, but Clara did not notice - she loved him instantly. He was *her* Nutcracker.

'Look,' said Fritz, 'that ugly Nutcracker can be the captain of my army,' and he ran through the crowded party to snatch the strange-looking wooden doll from his sister's hand. He jumped around, throwing the Nutcracker high into the air. 'You're the Nutcracker Captain! You're the Nutcracker Captain!' he chanted.

'Stop it, stop it! Don't hurt him!' shrieked Clara in despair as she chased her brother in and out of the throng.

When she finally managed to catch him, Fritz threw the Nutcracker on to the hard floor.

Clara was very angry with Fritz for treating her Nutcracker so badly. She was heartbroken to discover the doll's arm was broken, and began to cry. She did not mean to, but tears of anger and sadness rolled down her cheeks.

All the guests were watching Clara. So was the angel on top of the tree. Herr Drosselmeyer

tried to comfort his goddaughter by placing the doll's broken arm carefully in a sling. He told Clara to tuck the Nutcracker in the bed she kept for her favourite doll, and he would recover by morning.

Clara did as she was told, but could not believe it would do any good. Herr Drosselmeyer might be a magician, but would his special power be strong enough to mend her beloved Nutcracker?

Clara could not sleep. She thought of nothing but her broken doll. It was impossible to wait until morning to see him again so she crept very quietly downstairs. The huge room looked so strange now it was empty. The warm glow from the candles had been replaced by long fingers of grey shadow. The remains of the party feast lay on the table. The Christmas cake looked particularly delicious and just as she was cutting herself a slice Clara heard the whirring of the big grandfather clock in the corner. It was just about to strike.

If Clara had looked up she would have seen the Christmas angel smiling at her.

'Bong' went the clock, and Clara had the oddest of feelings.

'Bong ... ' She noticed the table was gradually getting bigger.

'Bong ... ' She looked around and saw the Christmas tree was growing too.

'Bong ... ' Everything in the room was becoming enormous, at least that's how it seemed to Clara.

In fact, Clara was shrinking – smaller and smaller.

The clock had struck twelve times. It was midnight.

Clara heard a scurrying noise behind her. She quickly moved to hide in the shadow cast by the enormous Christmas tree. She held her breath and listened as hard as she could. There it was again, but this time it was louder. Clara did not move a muscle as she saw a horde of mice, all as big as her, running into the room

from the direction of the fireplace. Clara thought they looked very unfriendly.

She counted at least twenty as they raced towards the table, and hurriedly began to help themselves to the cake Clara had been hoping to eat.

She tried to stay completely still but one of the mice spotted her and pointed her out to the others. They all charged towards her.

Clara was very frightened, but before the mice could run across the room, all Fritz's new toy soldiers came to life and formed themselves into a guard to protect her.

The mice continued to advance and very cleverly used their tails to trip the soldiers up. Clara was worried they were going to win.

Just as the situation looked hopeless, her beloved Nutcracker raced across the room from his bed, and took his place at the head of the column of soldiers. Clara was very relieved to see him. The Nutcracker showed the soldiers how to fire the cannon.

Very soon all the mice but one had been taken prisoner. The remaining mouse was the most terrifying of all. He was the Mouse King.

Clara watched in horror as the Mouse King tripped the Nutcracker with his long, snake-like tail.

'What can I do?' she thought. 'I can't let the Mouse King hurt my lovely Nutcracker.'

And in a rush of anger she took off her slipper, and threw it as hard as she could at the Mouse King.

Clara saw him stumble, but she did not see what happened next because at that moment the cannon fired with an earsplitting bang, and the room was filled with billowing grey smoke.

Clara coughed and had to shield her eyes from the stinging fumes. She wondered what

had happened to the Mouse King, and whether her precious Nutcracker was safe. She need not have worried!

As the cloud began to clear she peeped through the gaps in her fingers. She rubbed her eyes to make sure she was not dreaming. Then she realized it was all real. There in front of her was the most magical sight she had ever seen.

Beneath a round full moon the trees glis-
tened with freshly fallen snow. She looked
down and saw she was standing on ground
that sparkled as if sprinkled with diamonds.

Clara rubbed her eyes again in astonishment.
There was a sleigh and a pair of horses as white
as the snow. A handsome boy was holding
the reins.

'You have saved me from the Mouse King,'
said the boy as he stood up and gestured to

Clara to come and join him in the majestic
sleigh. 'To thank you I am going to take you
to my kingdom.' Clara looked at the boy's
eyes, and then at his clothes and realized to
her astonishment this was her beloved
Nutcracker.

'You have a kingdom?' she asked. Clara was
confused.

'I am the Prince of the Kingdom of Sweets,'
replied the Nutcracker Prince.

29

The Prince took the reins, and the sleigh sped through the twinkling stars.

Soon they came to a dazzling castle. The pair sat side-by-side on thrones encrusted with peppermint rock.

'We would like to welcome you back to your kingdom,' announced a very formal footman. 'We, your subjects, are delighted the evil spell of the Mouse King and Queen has been broken by the love of this beautiful young woman.'

Clara glanced at the Prince and could not stop smiling.

'In celebration of your safe return we have prepared an entertainment in your honour.'

Music played and the performance began. There were dancers from every land. First there was the Prince's favourite, the Sugar Plum Fairy. She enchanted Clara with her beautiful dress and magnificent pirouettes.

Then the Russian Cossacks threw their legs up so high, Clara thought they would fall over. She had never seen such colourful costumes. The ladies wore feathers and ribbons in their hair. The men had big hats that made Clara laugh. She had never been so happy.

When she had stopped laughing the Prince turned to her and bowed.

'Would you give me the honour of the next dance?' he asked.

He swept her onto the floor and they danced from one end of the room to the other and back again. Everyone agreed they looked wonderful together.

Clara danced until her feet could not move another step.

She sat wearily on her throne and felt her eyes gently closing. She loved watching the dancing, but try as she might she could not keep her eyes open any longer. The music and laughter of the dancers became fainter and fainter as she drifted into a happy sleep.

Suddenly there was a knock at the door. Clara woke up with a start. She was very surprised to find herself sitting by the Christmas tree at home. She rubbed the sleep from her eyes.

'Where is my Nutcracker Prince?' Clara wondered, and she looked around the deserted room.

The knock at the door was louder this time. Then the door swung open and Clara saw the visitor was her godfather.

'May I come in?' he asked.

As she closed the door, she felt very bewildered.

'I have come specially to thank you, dear Clara,' Herr Drosselmeyer said with his kindly smile.

'What for?' asked Clara innocently.

'My nephew has come back. He is the best Christmas present I could ever have.'

Before Clara had time to gather her thoughts, there was another knock.

'Happy Christmas Clara!' announced the Nutcracker Prince.

Clara could not say anything. She was speechless with happiness.

Herr Drosselmeyer glanced up at the smiling angel on top of the Christmas tree. The angel knew everyone was going to have the best Christmas imaginable.